Reinhard Bonnke

First of all ... Intercession

Prayer
Intercessio
Praye

Intercession
English

ISBN 3-935057-17-2

Edition 4, Printing 2
6,000 copies

Originally Published by CfaN 1996
ISBN 3-931831-01-9

Cover design by Isabelle Brasche
Cover photographs by Peter van den Berg & Corel Graphics Suite
Typeset by Adrian Bradshaw

Published by:

E-R Productions LLC
P.O. Box 593647
Orlando, FL 32859
USA

info@e-r-productions.com
www.e-r-productions.com

Visit the CfaN website at
www.CfaN.org

Printed in Brazil

FIRST OF ALL ... INTERCESSION

I exhort first of all that supplications, prayers, intercessions, and giving of thanks be made for all men. (1 Timothy 2:1)

1

THE SILENT PLANET

Why do we need prayer? In the beginning Adam and Eve did not pray in the sense in which most of us would understand prayer today. God and man seemed to enjoy almost family openness. God was 'the Voice' walking in the garden in the cool of the day.

Then the party broke up. Relations became strained and distant. C. S. Lewis described this world as 'the silent planet' – silent toward heaven. Earth hung in space like a spiritual black hole, which gave no light.

Psalm 14:2-3 says:

> *The LORD looks down from heaven upon the children of men, to see if there are any who understand, who seek God. They have all turned aside, they have together become corrupt; There is none who does good, No, not one.*

Think of what happens to a country at war; in some cases it is totally cut off from the outside world. There is no more commerce or trade, no more mail or telephone conversations. Much the same thing happened when the human race surrendered to sin and the devil. We were cut off from the outside world – from God, from the world of the Spirit. Demonic forces occupied this world and dominated our attitudes. Divine power lines were severed and a permanent spiritual blackout occurred.

Originally, God put man in charge to manage this world, but we were a pushover to sin and the devil swayed people as Rasputin swayed the Czar of Russia. The Bible makes this clear:

> *The whole world lies under the sway of the wicked one.* (1 John 5:19)
>
> *Their foolish hearts were darkened.* (Romans 1:21)
>
> *The prince of the power of the air, the spirit who now works in the sons of disobedience.* (Ephesians 2:2)
>
> *Alienated and enemies in your mind by wicked works.* (Colossians 1:21)

Three times Jesus called the devil *the ruler of this world* (John 12:31, 14:30, 16:11). When the devil offered the kingdoms of this world to Christ, Jesus did not contest the devil's ability to do so (Matthew 4:8-9).

COUNTERATTACK

God's wisdom permitted this state of affairs, because He had counter plans. Just as in wartime countries have secret agents and the means of maintaining contact with them, so the Lord had His men and women and kept in contact with them. Amos the prophet said, "*Surely the Lord GOD does nothing, unless He reveals His secret to His servants the prophets*" (Amos 3:7) – men like Enoch, Noah, Abraham, Moses, Elijah, Daniel, and Isaiah. The whole nation of Israel was to have been God's ally against the occupying enemy from hell, but they failed to perceive His plan and comply with it.

The Lord revealed one great secret to His servants the prophets, namely that there was to be an invasion of fortress Earth from the outside. It took place. Christ came to the shores of Satan's usurped dominion proclaiming the Kingdom of God and displaying its power. "*But if I cast out demons with the finger of God, surely the kingdom of God has come upon you*" (Luke 11:20).

STRATEGIC WEAPONRY

Christians have a world to reclaim and regain for God. The enemy has brought about vast destruction, death, and wickedness. Prayer opens up God's armory with its superior weapons. If we think that we do not need to pray, then we do not know what we are up against. If we think that we can manage on our own achievements, then we simply make

Christians have a world to reclaim and regain for God.

ourselves the devil's laughing stock. Prayerless means defenseless. Cleverness and science are like a feather duster against a tank. The unlimited greatness of the Cross is needed against the cosmic evil.

Prayer and intercession cast out the entrenched enemy, violate his borders, and retake lost territory. The devil hates this kind of prayer. Praying is not meditative retirement, breathing 'the still dews of quietness till all our strivings cease.' It is heaven's militancy. It is not a muttered litany but a top C soul-shriek. Prayer is an aggressive multipurpose weapon put in our hands by God to overcome every kind of satanic resistance. The person who prays overleaps human limits. Believers are authorized to go to the counter of heaven's supplies store for superhuman resources.

The person who prays overleaps human limits.

THE NEW AND LIVING WAY

The coming of Christ was the beginning of the end for the devil. The spiritual advance goes on today. The armies of God form a new race of men and women, a holy nation, born again, presenting the Word of God with faith and prayer. We have new access to God, a new method of operation and new authority, *by a new and living way*, through Christ Jesus (Hebrews 10:20). Victory is assured. *The creation itself also will be delivered from the bondage of corruption into the glorious liberty of the children of God … for we were saved in this hope* (Romans 8:21,24).

Why live as if we were not on speaking terms with the Lord? He dwells with us. We are not mere neighbors, living with a brick wall between us. The Lord has broken down the middle wall. We have been *brought near by the blood of Christ* (Ephesians 2:13). The Christian life means life with God, with everything centered on Him, God-orientated. The Holy Spirit gives us *utterance* to get through to God (Acts 2:4).

Christ's model prayer ends with – *For Yours is the kingdom and the power and the glory forever* (Matthew 6:13). God's is the power, ours is the prayer. Prayer is necessary, not just nice – a vital part of the equation. Ezekiel the prophet pictures the currents of the Spirit as waters to swim in (Ezekiel 47). The Lord provides the waters, but we do the swimming. Without prayer we are not 'in the swim' at all.

2

ALL PRAYER

Turn over each page of the New Testament and mark every prayer reference. Then you will see how prayer is emphasized. In the first Gospel alone, there are 41 references and 230 throughout the New Testament, some of them extensive, with 10 different words for prayer. We read there about *praying always with ALL prayer* (Ephesians 6:18). There are different methods, forms, and moods, yet all of them available for man to use against the devil.

Some texts use one special word like a hammer to drive the nail in deep. The adverb 'without ceasing' (Greek ektenes = constant, adialeiptos = without ceasing) comes only six times in Scripture and only about prayer, as if this were the one thing never to let up.

> *Peter was therefore kept in prison, but constant prayer was offered to God for him by the church.* (Acts 12:5)
>
> *Without ceasing I make mention of you always in my prayers.* (Romans 1:9)
>
> *We give thanks to God always for you all, making mention of you in our prayers, remembering without ceasing your work of faith.* (1 Thessalonians 1:2-3)
>
> *We also thank God without ceasing.* (1 Thessalonians 2:13)
>
> *Pray without ceasing.* (1 Thessalonians 5:17)
>
> *Without ceasing I remember you in my prayers night and day.* (2 Timothy 1:3)

Jesus Himself taught that *men always ought to pray and not lose heart* (Luke 18:1).

Another set of examples shows the use of a word meaning 'keep at it, persevere, be a stayer, show stamina, stick at it, keep awake!' Translate these texts like that yourself:

> *Continue earnestly in prayer, being vigilant in it with thanksgiving.* (Colossians 4:2)

Continuing steadfastly in prayer.
(Romans 12:12)

We will give ourselves continually to prayer.
(Acts 6:4)

Praying always with all prayer and supplication in the Spirit, being watchful to this end with all perseverance and supplication for all the saints.
(Ephesians 6:18)

The way that Jesus speaks of prayer is not quite like some suppose. He said, "*Ask, and it will be given to you … seek … knock*" (Matthew 7:7). These words are in the Greek present indicative – be asking, be seeking, be knocking. But elsewhere He used a different tense (aorist) indicating a single, completed action – "*Give us this day our daily bread*" (Matthew 6:11). Ask once, but every day, "*Give us this day.*" Ask for each day's need daily. That is how God likes it, not 'having faith' for everything for a whole year, but coming to Him as children over and over, asking for the bread of life, and the Holy Spirit, daily, not once forever. We always receive every day.

GOD HEARS PRAYER

Scripture consistently declares that prayer will always be heard.

Your Father knows the things you have need of before you ask Him. (Matthew 6:8)

Everyone who asks receives, and he who seeks finds, and to him who knocks it will be opened. (Matthew 7:8)

Now this is the confidence that we have in Him, that if we ask anything according to His will, He hears us. And if we know that He hears us, whatever we ask, we know that we have the petitions that we have asked of Him. (1 John 5:14-15)

3

FOLLOWING THE RULES

To pray, simply follow the ground rules. There are conditions, but none that are impossible to fulfill.

1. Ask in faith in God (Matthew 21:22; James 1:6). We cannot ask too much and blow a fuse by overloading the demand on divine help. "Ask!" That is Christ's command, so you cannot be outside the will of God by asking, but you can if you do not ask.

2. Do not come apologetically in case you are asking inappropriately or outside God's will. Our job is to ask anyway, and let God decide how to act. It will not upset God, whatever we ask. We can worry so much about God's will that we never have any faith at all or maybe never pray! We have made it such a mark of high piety to ask only for what God wants that it contradicts what Jesus said in John 15:7: "*Ask what you desire, and it shall be done for you.*" God allows mature believers free choice over large areas of their lives – and blesses what they decide.

3. Forgive as God forgives you (Mark 11:25; Luke 6:37; Matthew 5:23-24).

4. Do not pray *to be heard of men,* but sincerely – not as was said of one preacher "his prayer was the most eloquent ever delivered to a New York congregation." Remember God is full of grace (Luke 18:10-14).

5. Pray in the name of Jesus (John 14:13, 16:23). Since we are in Christ, one with Him, when we pray in the name of Jesus, we are speaking with Christ's merits imputed to us. Common sense says we cannot ask, "In the name of Jesus, help me rob my neighbor!" Two women who wrote to a preacher overlooked this and said, "We are praying for your death. We have been successful in two previous cases!"

6. Cherish the word of God. Notice the balance of this sentence: "*If you abide in Me, and My words abide in you, you will ask what you desire, and it shall be done for you*" (John 15:7). "*If I regard iniquity in my heart, the Lord will not hear*" (Psalm 66:18). Treasure the word of Christ; do not cherish iniquity.

7. Deal with obstacles to answered prayer. James warns why many times we may not be heard. *But let him ask in faith, with no doubting, for he who doubts is like a wave of the sea driven and tossed by the wind. For let not that man suppose that he will receive anything from the Lord* (James 1:6-7). *You ask and do not receive, because you ask amiss, that you may spend it on your pleasures* (James 4:3).

Jesus prayed, "*not My will, but Yours, be done.*" (Luke 22:42). We are not all-wise and do not make perfect petitions. If we had the management of omnipotence (unlimited power), we would soon make a mess of things. God, however, will not be persuaded to do what is folly – not even to please somebody. His answers are wiser than our prayers – even His "Nos!"

It used to be taught that King Hezekiah (Isaiah 38) prayed for longer life, and God gave him another 15 years, but against His will because during those 15 years Manasseh, Hezekiah's son, was born and for over 50 years led the nation into wickedness. But in fact, if Hezekiah had died without a son, the Davidic line to Christ as chronicled in Matthew chapter 1 would have come to a premature end. God does nothing against His will – pray on!

God does nothing against His will – pray on!

4

KNOWING GOD

Above everything else, know the Lord. How easy it is to ask the wrong person for the things we need! But we do not usually ask a plumber for medicine or a doctor to repair a water pipe. Know who God is. Do not address a vague Somebody somewhere up in the stratosphere, with no idea of who He is or how He might react. Do not be like the liberal preacher who thought of God as 'a kind of oblong blur,' or like the Athenians with an altar to the unknown God (Acts 17:22-23). Some people even talk of "seeking the unknown."

That kind of mystical nonsense is like begging from any passer-by, hoping to chance on a billionaire. But it is better to know a billionaire. To recognize God's true identity always encourages more intelligent and more effective praying. God is our Father.

What kind of reaction can we expect if we treat God as an 'oblong blur'? The Almighty has made almighty efforts to tell us about Himself, even sending Jesus Christ. To ignore what He says involves a deliberate and dangerous resolution to remain in ignorance, exactly what we might expect when the devil influences us. To brush aside the greatest spiritual knowledge ever revealed is suicidal. Even God Himself can do nothing more for us then.

Recognizing God's true identity encourages more intelligent and effective praying.

People question why, if God is all-powerful, He does not do this or that. But God is not only all-powerful, but also all-wise, holy, and just. Furthermore He has His own prior plans, not likely to be changed for one of our impulses. You do not ask a surgeon performing an operation to make you a cup of tea. We must at least flow in the direction of the divine stream.

Know God, His ways, His counsel, His character! All His attributes are laid open in His Word. Read it! This is the secret of so many Christians' wonderful faith and confidence, their path to God guided by Scripture.

The book of James, largely about prayer, speaks of God's goodness as always shining like the sun. *Every good gift and every perfect gift is from above, and comes down from the Father of lights, with whom there is no variation or shadow of turning* (James 1:17). This picture is a sundial, which registers the sun's movement by its shadow. When there is no shadow, it is noon, because the sun is at the zenith and casts no shadow. God never casts a shadow because He is always at the zenith. He never varies, changes, or declines. For everybody He is always the same prayer-answering God.

5

THE NEW WAY

The first Christians crossed the Bible landscape in an aura of prayer. They reveled in prayer, and with good reason. Their kind of praying was a new thing, using the name of Jesus. The New Testament speaks of *fellowship with the Father,* but Israel did not pray "Our Father." They had such a lofty conception of God that He seemed unapproachable, the Sovereign Lord of Hosts, mighty in battle, or at best a present help in trouble.

Only an elite band enjoyed God's company and intimate prayer life with Him. Most knew God only second-hand, via a priest or prophet. In a sense, people called on the Lord in their own name. *Lord, remember David* (Psalm 132:1), hoping for personal favor.

"OUR FATHER"

We should all seek to perceive God's true position; He is infinitely superior to us. But the invitation to call Him Father brings Him close to us and makes Him approachable. Readers of the book of Hebrews, still emerging from the old dispensation, had to be taken by the hand, and led into this new relationship. They were told:

Calling God "Father" makes Him approachable.

> *Seeing then that we have a great High Priest … Jesus the Son of God … let us therefore come boldly to the throne of grace … having boldness to enter the Holiest by the blood of Jesus, by a new and living way which He consecrated for us, through the veil, that is, His flesh.*
> (Hebrews 4:14-16, 10:19-20)

When Jesus taught His disciples to pray, it made them a new breed, praying always and about everything. He had told them "*Most assuredly, I say to you, whatever you ask the Father in My name He will give you … ask, and you will receive*" (John 16:23-24). In a way, to call on God is instinctive. Who does not – especially when in distress? But Christ taught us the right way to go about it – to pray in His name. His mighty works mark a new road to God. He has opened heaven's door. Enter! We will be received.

REVELING IN PRAYER

The quotations above are part of an astonishing New Testament array of similar references to prayer. The main word for prayer (Greek proseuche, proseuchomai) is used over 120 times. God gives many things without being asked – rain, sunshine, winter, and summer – but He planned that we should receive other things by asking for them. The list is long and includes salvation, the Holy Spirit, guidance, equipment for spiritual battles, the Gifts of the Spirit, power to witness, strength, effectiveness, boldness, relief from anxieties, anti-devil weapons, our 'daily bread', the kingdom to come, the will of God to be done, relief from trial and temptation, healing – and more. We are even to pray for our enemies.

Communicating with God is the Christian distinction. Jesus forbad '*vain repetition*,' like bowing five times a day declaring that God is great. The disciples opened their hearts to God about everything, including their innermost feelings. For example, they wrote letters in the style of those days but changed the usual good wishes and pleasantries into prayers. Paul wrote to Christians in Rome, "*Without ceasing I make mention of you always in my prayers*" (Romans 1:9). To believers in Corinth, Galatia, Ephesus, Philippi, Colosse, Thessalonica, and to Timothy, he wrote: "*Grace to you and peace from God our Father and the Lord Jesus Christ.*" Some letters appear to be just extended prayers. Augustine wrote his immortal book 'Confessions' as a letter to God.

"If wishes were horses, beggars would ride," it is said, but the first Christians addressed wishes to the Father in the name of Jesus and did ride. Praise God! The unbeliever wishes, the believer prays. In Acts 27:29, the soldiers and crew of a ship were in danger and 'wished for daybreak'. Paul prayed, and they were saved.

James 'wished' in the Christian way: "*Pray* (wish) *for one another that you may be healed*" (James 5:16). Like John writing to Gaius, "*I pray* (wish) *that you may prosper in all things and be in health*" (3 John 2). Wishes become prayers and answers are expected. The unbeliever sighs, "If only ..." The believer rejoices *in hope of the glory of God* (Romans 5:2).

6

INTERCESSION

Intercession is a special form of prayer for believers. But what exactly does it involve?

1. A special assignment for believers

Believers are called to a special work, not just to ask for things for themselves but also to stand before God for others. This is a vital feature of the superstructure of world redemption. Christ is the great Intercessor, and we are called to a similar role. Christ's intercessory work is on a different level from ours, but He is still our role model.

2. Dual knowledge

Intercession needs knowledge of those for whom we intercede and of the One to whom we address our prayers. Jesus took our nature on Himself and also carried the nature of God in perfection – He was fully human and fully divine. He identified Himself with us and with God. We are human, but have received the *divine nature* (2 Peter 1:4). We have kinship with both God and man. And so we are fitted for the work to which God has appointed us.

3. Christ-like compassion

However, we need more if we are to enter into true intercession. Our role model, Jesus, poured out a flood of compassion. This was His sole motivating force. The effective power of intercession derives from a spontaneous outflow of concern and love. Generally speaking, it is naturally there for our own family and friends. Now it must embrace all the world.

SOME EXAMPLES

Although the Christian basis of prayer is not in the Old Testament, it is there that we find the great examples of intercession. Abraham interceded for Abimelech, and for the doomed cities of Sodom and Gomorrah. Moses, Solomon, Elijah, Hezekiah, Daniel, Ezra, Esther, Jeremiah, and the prophets interceded for the nation of Israel. There are even intercessory Psalms.

As an evangelist I am called to stand before very big crowds, but I dare not preach unless I know that intercessory prayer has ascended for those very people. Workers go out to the crusade area in advance and spend several weeks there, specifically to prepare the ground through intercession. Christians are recruited locally and instructed to storm heaven with pleadings for the souls of men and women. Indeed, when these teams of intercessors hammer on the door of glory, it adds weight to the prayers of tens of thousands of people around the whole world that the souls of those in the crowd may be delivered and saved.

During our evangelistic crusades, a spirit of prayer and intercession soaks my soul and often makes me jump out of bed at 3 o'clock in the morning. Hundreds, sometimes thousands, of intercessors uphold me in prayer while I am ministering on the platform. This provides my spirit with lift like a powerful thermal for an eagle. I glance across a sea of faces and rejoice that the devil's hand has been struck off their shoulders.

In western churches comparatively few unbelievers venture to expose themselves to evangelism. Usually, they are brought to a meeting by somebody who has sought God on their behalf – perhaps for years. The ground is already watered with tears and prepared. What about the teeming populations of Africa, Asia, China, India, Japan, and Indonesia? How many are ever named personally before the Lord? These great unprayed for masses are struggling human beings like ourselves, however remotely acquainted we are with them. If we do not intercede for them, who will?

In the darkness of a bedeviled world, our prayers cut the darkness like lasers, becoming channels through which God's blessing may reach earth, and transmitting the power-currents of Calvary and the Resurrection. Intercession jams the wavelengths of the devil. Certainly the devil will resist and the world will howl in protest, too long undisturbed. The works of Satan are many, but they must go. *For this purpose the Son of God was manifested, that He might destroy the works of the devil* (1 John 3:8).

Intercession honors those for whom we pray, better than recommending them for the Honors List. In 2 Kings 4, we read about a great woman. She is called great, but she was not famous and did not want to be. She gave quiet hospitality to Elisha the prophet, and to thank her, he asked, "*Do you want me to speak on your behalf to the king or to the commander of the army?*" (2 Kings 4:13). "No!" she said. High circles did not attract her, but she did want Elisha to name her to God. He did so, and this began the thrilling miracle story of the birth of her son, his death, and his being raised to life again. Elisha named her to the Lord, and it brought her immortal fame.

Praying brings distinction to ourselves and to those for whom we pray.

Praying brings distinction to ourselves and to those for whom we pray. It highlights them, makes nobodies somebodies before God. He turns His attention to them – just imagine that! *I sought for a man among them who would make a wall, and stand in the gap before Me on behalf of the land, that I should not destroy it; but I found no one* (Ezekiel 22:30). Politicians, talkers, musicians, but not one intercessor. If He had found a man, his name would be in the Book, immortalized. To intercede means we join an elite company notable in heaven.

It may be the only practical thing we can do for some people. Elisha could only pray for his hostess. To omit prayer from our activities is loveless, grieving the Spirit of God. Samuel looked at wayward Israel and said, "*You have done all this wickedness … far be it from me that I should sin against the* LORD *in ceasing to pray for you*" (1 Samuel 12:20, 23).

HEART-CRY

To God, nobody is a nobody. Each individual has a value beyond computation. Our prayers should be in direct proportion to the desperate wickedness from which people need saving. The worse the wickedness, the more the intercession. Nobody should have to go through life without somebody praying for him (or her).

Let me ask you to read this from 1 Timothy 2:1-4:

> *Therefore I exhort first of all that supplications, prayers, intercessions, and giving of thanks be made FOR ALL men, for kings and all who are in authority, that we may lead a quiet and peaceable life in all godliness and reverence. For this is good and acceptable in the sight of God our Savior, who desires all men to be saved and to come to the knowledge of the truth.*

So, the ultimate aim of intercession is evangelism – God *desires all men to be saved.* Intercession is not a say-so, but a heart-cry. Not "Lord, bless me and everybody everywhere. Amen!" Our Lord Jesus prayed for us until He sweat drops of blood. He even prayed for the soldiers hammering nails through his quivering flesh.

Pray for all men, for Christlessness is terrible. There is only one Savior, and if He is rejected what can people do? Their cry is like Reuben's when he found Joseph had gone: "*And I, where shall I go?*" (Genesis 37:30). There is nowhere to go. So, people just drift along, perhaps together, unknowingly heading for a Sargasso Sea called hell. Christless religion is hell on earth. Religious leaders killed Christ. We see it today in unbridled hate, terrorism, murder, and oppression in the name of God. Jesus said, "*If you were Abraham's children, you would do the works of Abraham. But now you seek to kill Me … Abraham did not do this. You are of your father the devil … he was a murderer from the beginning.*" (John 8:39-44) Intercession is urgent. Intercession brings divine intervention. We have one generation in which to save a generation, not a century.

Our Lord Jesus prayed for us until He sweat drops of blood.

Alfred, Lord Tennyson only told half the truth when he wrote, "More things are wrought by prayer than this world dreams of." The other half is this – more things are not handled in prayer than this world dreams of. We live dangerously, leaving many important matters out of our prayers. Unanswered prayers are usually the ones that were never prayed, but interceding for the salvation of the nations receives immediate attention. It touches the heart-interest of God.

7

HOW TO BECOME A TRUE INTERCESSOR

1. A true intercessor must have some standing with both parties.

As I have already written (page 18), we know people, but we must also know God! Abraham is a good example of someone who knew God. The cities of Sodom and Gomorrah had become morally perverted so God proposed to remove them. He said, "*Shall I hide from Abraham what I am doing?*" (Genesis 18:17) When Abraham learned that these two cities were listed for destruction, he took up their case with God and went a long way along the road to saving them. He was qualified because he knew God – and the cities.

He was called the friend of God (2 Chronicles 20:7; Isaiah 41:8). Why? *Abraham believed God, and it was accounted to him for righteousness. And he was called the friend of God* (James 2:23). Believers – I do not mean unbelieving believers full of doubts, asking clever questions, but men and women of living faith, who know the Lord – are the King's friends at court, his confidants, people to whom He listens and with whom He wants to cooperate. They are to be His intercessors.

That is what Scripture means by a friend. Jesus said, "*No longer do I call you servants … but I have called you friends, for all things that I heard from My Father I have made known to you*" (John 15:15). A friend-intercessor will have the mind of the Lord, who tells us nothing for mere interest but for us to pray about it. A word of knowledge is not necessarily for public consumption but for private prayer. God reveals what He will do to those who clamor for His will to be done.

After a campaign meeting a lady came to me and told me how she had been "molested by evil spirits for very many years" and how she despaired of life. I was moved by what she said, and I promised to pray for her. When I reached my hotel, the Lord told me to fast and pray for her. I did so. The next day I was praying for her with all of my heart, when at noon I suddenly experienced a breakthrough. The glory of the Lord filled my soul and the Holy Spirit said to me, "It is done." That evening I met the lady again. Before I could say anything, she said with shining eyes, "God has done the miracle. Today at noon, I experienced a mighty deliverance at my home." What God does on a small scale, he will also do on the largest.

2. A true intercessor is moved by feelings of concern.

The story in Exodus chapter 32 is a strange episode, but shows us the heart of a true intercessor. Moses was angry over Israel's idolatry. Israel had escaped from Egypt after a fantastic display of omnipotence that would make God seem physically near. Above them towered Mount Sinai, with the cloud of God's glory concealing Moses, who had ascended to speak with

God. The people thought he had deserted them. Their simple minds were soaked in the superstitions of Egypt and its gods, and so they made a golden calf to lead them back to Egypt.

The Lord said He would put an end to them because of this appalling lapse and begin a new nation through Moses. Moses' first reaction was to send swordsmen to rid Israel of the ringleaders. Then his pity overcame his anger and he besought God to save the nation God called "*a stiff-necked people*" (Exodus 32:9). Moses called them "*Your people*" (verse 11) and pleaded, "*Oh, these people have committed a great sin … yet now, if You will forgive their sin – but if not, I pray, blot me out of Your book which You have written*" (Exodus 32:31-32). Here words failed him, such was the force of his compassionate outburst. He offered to die as an atonement for Israel's sin. His offer was turned down because only the Son of God could atone for sin. But this is an example of true intercession.

This proposal was unsolicited. Moses had not been pushed into it. He had brought this rabble of tribes to nationhood like a woman bringing a child into the world. They broke his heart but he still defended them from the inevitable disaster of their own folly.

We pray for Christian revival. Why? To see the church full, pay the bills, ease the labors of evangelism, as a religious duty? Look at the pitiful attempts of Christless people to save themselves, making their own impotent gods. Let us weep for them. Let us cry out to God (Joel 1:13-14, 2:12-13). God is moved when our hearts – not just our mouths – are moved.

3. A true intercessor has faith.

All the great prayers of intercession in Scripture were triggered heavenward from the launch pad of faith. Faith is assurance of the changeless character of God's goodness, believing He is faithful to what He says He is. If prayer is controversial, then everything is. If all answers to prayer were printed, they would fill the Atlantic depths.

Faith is faith in God, not just in a miracle happening. The great Bible intercessors did not always see what they asked for. God heard Abraham, but in the end the cities of Sodom and Gomorrah were destroyed. Pray on and leave matters in God's hands to do whatever He knows is good.

4. A true intercessor delights in praise and worship.

Throughout the intercessory Psalms, there is not a single instance of honor to God being omitted in some shape or form. The one psalm of unrelieved gloom, Psalm 88, makes no petition and offers no praise. But intercession rises to God on the wings of worship. Requests and praise are two sides of the same coin.

> *Be anxious for nothing, but in everything by prayer and supplication, with thanksgiving, let your requests be made known to God.* (Philippians 4:6)
>
> *As you have therefore received Christ Jesus the Lord, so walk in Him … abounding in it with thanksgiving. Continue earnestly in prayer, being vigilant in it with thanksgiving.* (Colossians 2:6-7, 4:2)

> *Rejoice always, pray without ceasing, in everything give thanks; for this is the will of God in Christ Jesus for you.*
> (1 Thessalonians 5:16-18)

> *Let the hearts of those rejoice who seek the* *LORD!* (Psalm 105:3)

Intercessors do not come to God being offended about what He has not done. Moaning is not praying. Our burden for the world's needs is lifted as we pray in remembrance and thanks for what He can – and will – do.

The Lord's Prayer begins "*Our Father, hallowed be your name.*" That is the beginning of all true intercession, and the end is "*for Yours is the kingdom and power and the glory for ever and ever. Amen.*"

Other books & bookle

The Holy Spirit Baptism

The greatest assurance of all flows from personal experience of the manifestation of God's power. Drawing from Scripture, this carefully explained and simple to understand booklet brings the believer to the place of faith where he or she can receive the Baptism of the Holy Spirit. Common misconceptions are answered and the reader is challenged to ask and receive!

32 pages • ISBN 3-935057-12-1 .

How to have Assurance of Salvation

This booklet tackles the first and most vital crisis that every new believer faces. Before anything else, we must know we are saved! It is the crucial link between salvation and discipleship. Using graphic illustrations from Scripture, this message forms the basis of the booklet *Now that You are Saved*, given to new believers in every CfaN campaign.

28 pages • ISBN 3-935057-11-3

First of all ... Intercession

"Evangelism without intercession is like an explosive without a detonator," says Reinhard Bonnke. Christians have a world to reclaim and regain for God. Prayer and intercession cast out the entrenched enemy, violate his borders and retake lost territory. This booklet explains the task of intercession clearly and concisely, and encourages Christians to use the weapon of prayer more consistently and effectively.

32 pages • ISBN 3-935057-17-2

The Secret of the Power of the Blood of Jesus

The blood type of Jesus is unique. Since it was spiritually created it has spiritual power. As a young evangelist Reinhard Bonnke vowed that wherever he went he would preach on the blood of Jesus. This booklet contains that powerful gospel message in all its life-changing anointing.

24 pages • ISBN 3-935057-10-5

Reinhard Bonnke

The Coming One

Now that we are in the third millennium, millions of people are still looking for a great global leader. They even consult the stars looking for a new age under a super-personality to bring accord between the races, peace among the nations, and the rich caring for the poor. Christ declared that He would come back, and He will! This is the key hope of every Christian creed. The last prayer of the Bible is Amen! Come Lord Jesus!

28 pages • ISBN 3-935057-84-9

How to receive a Miracle from God

Perhaps the greatest single obstacle to accepting the reality of miracles is our inability to understand God's dynamics. The dynamics of the miraculous are the Word of God, Faith, and Obedience. When these three are in place, miracles happen. This booklet will unlock the doors of unbelieving hearts to expect a miracle from God.

24 pages • ISBN 3-935057-13-X

The Lord Your Healer

God loves to heal. He still heals today. During CfaN campaigns, we see thousands receive healing and remain totally healed. This straight forward but profound booklet answers the critics and lifts our faith. We do not look to church leaders, special ministries or Reinhard Bonnke for healing, but to Jesus. He will answer.

24 pages • ISBN 3-935057-14-8

The Romance of Redeeming Love

When God gave his Son Jesus to die for us, it cost Him everything. The gift of Redemption is the ultimate expression of God's love. This booklet reveals through Scripture, God's unique and perfect Redemption plan. Creation was easy, but for our Redemption, God gave Himself.

32 pages • ISBN 3-935057-15-6

Evangelism by Fire
Igniting your passion for the lost

"This book is not only mighty, but it is meaty! It will rekindle the corners of your soul and turn its center to a white-hot focus on what matters most to God - the salvation and deliverance of eternal souls. Bonnke's words have a way of bringing you to that altar anew - to be baptized with Jesus' fire once again."

Jack W. Hayford, D. Litt.

320 pages • 16 page color photo section • ISBN 3-935057-19-9
Supporting **Workbook & Study Guide** available • ISBN 3-935057-28-8

Mighty Manifestations
The Gifts and Power of the Holy Spirit

A book to challenge the believer to step out and use the 'power tools of God', the gifts of the Holy Spirit. All the gifts are covered in detail. Reinhard Bonnke shows how we can be effective in using the gifts we have been given.

248 pages • 16 page color photo section • ISBN 3-935057-00-8
Supporting **Workbook & Study Guide** available • ISBN 3-935057-27-X

Faith ... the Link with God's Power

Reinhard Bonnke draws from his years of personal study and ministry to millions to reveal that Faith is the fertile ground in which God moves and it is not the size of your faith, but the size of your God you believe in that determines the results. Faith is like a wiring system that carries power into our lives. Faith itself is not the power, but it links us to the power source. There is no link to God's power without faith.

346 pages • 16 page color photo section • ISBN 3-935057-29-6
Supporting **Workbook & Study Guide** available • ISBN 3-935057-26-1

Time is Running Out

With his passionate desire to see souls won for Christ, Reinhard expounds the biblical principles of successful evangelism. Proven and effective techniques for reaching the lost are skillfully, yet simply, described, in order to teach, inspire, and encourage others to take up the challenge to reach out to their neighbors, friends, and the world.

In just 3 years, after preaching face to face to over 31 million people, over 20 million of them made a positive decision for Jesus Christ, and have been added to the Kingdom of God and to the local churches.

288 pages •16 page color photo section • ISBN 3-935057-60-1
Supporting **Workbook & Study Guide** available • ISBN 3-935057-85-7